# Roc

## Greek Philosopher and Disciple of Jesus

## By Twelve Midwayers
[Paper 160 and Paper 161 of The Urantia Book]

## Paper 160
## Rodan of Alexandria

160:0.1 (1772.1) ON SUNDAY morning, September 18, Andrew announced that no work would be planned for the coming week. All of the apostles, except Nathaniel and Thomas, went home to visit their families or to sojourn with friends. This week Jesus enjoyed a period of almost complete rest, but Nathaniel and Thomas were very busy with their discussions with a certain Greek philosopher from Alexandria named Rodan. This Greek had recently become a disciple of Jesus through the teaching of one of Abner's associates who had conducted a mission at Alexandria. Rodan was now earnestly engaged in the task of harmonizing his philosophy of life with Jesus' new religious teachings, and he had come to Magadan hoping that the Master would talk these problems over with him. He also desired to secure a firsthand and authoritative version of the gospel from either Jesus or one of his apostles. Though the Master declined to enter into such a conference with Rodan, he did receive him graciously and immediately directed that Nathaniel and Thomas should listen to all he had to say and tell him about the gospel in return.

1. Rodan's Greek Philosophy

160:1.1 (1772.2) Early Monday morning,

Rodan began a series of ten addresses to Nathaniel, Thomas, and a group of some two dozen believers who chanced to be at Magadan. These talks, condensed, combined, and restated in modern phraseology, present the following thoughts for consideration:

160:1.2 (1772.3) Human life consists in three great drives—urges, desires, and lures. Strong character, commanding personality, is only acquired by converting the natural urge of life into the social art of living, by transforming present desires into those higher longings which are capable of lasting attainment, while the commonplace lure of existence must be transferred from one's conventional and established ideas to the higher realms of unexplored ideas and undiscovered ideals.

160:1.3 (1772.4) The more complex civilization becomes, the more difficult will become the art of living. The more rapid the changes in social usage, the more complicated will become the task of character development. Every ten generations mankind must learn anew the art of living if progress is to continue. And if man becomes so ingenious that he more rapidly adds to the complexities of society, the art of living will need to be remastered in less time, perhaps every single generation. If the evolution of the art of living fails to keep pace with the technique of existence, humanity will quickly revert to the simple urge of living—the attainment of the satisfaction of present desires. Thus will humanity remain immature; society will fail in growing up to full maturity.

160:1.4 (1773.1) Social maturity is equivalent to the degree to which man is willing to surrender the gratification of mere transient and present desires for the entertainment of those superior longings the striving for whose attainment affords the more abundant satisfactions of progressive advancement toward permanent goals. But the true badge of social maturity is the willingness of a people to surrender the right to live peaceably and contentedly under the ease-promoting standards of the lure of established beliefs and conventional ideas for the disquieting and energy-requiring lure of the pursuit of the unexplored possibilities of the attainment of undiscovered goals of idealistic spiritual realities.

160:1.5 (1773.2) Animals respond nobly to the urge of life, but only man can attain the art of living, albeit the majority of mankind only experience the animal urge to live. Animals know only this blind and instinctive urge; man is capable of transcending this urge to natural function. Man may elect to live upon the high plane of intelligent art, even that of celestial joy and spiritual ecstasy. Animals make no inquiry into the purposes of life; therefore they never worry, neither do they commit suicide. Suicide among men testifies that such beings have emerged from the purely animal stage of existence, and to the further fact that the exploratory efforts of such human beings have failed to attain the artistic levels of mortal experience. Animals know not the meaning of life; man not only possesses capacity for the recognition of values and the comprehension of meanings, but he also is conscious of the meaning of meanings—he is self-conscious of insight.

160:1.6 (1773.3) When men dare to forsake a life of natural craving for one of adventurous art and uncertain logic, they must expect to suffer the consequent hazards of emotional casualties— conflicts, unhappiness, and uncertainties—at least until the time of their attainment of some degree of intellectual and emotional maturity. Discouragement, worry, and indolence are positive evidence of moral immaturity. Human society is confronted with two problems: attainment of the maturity of the individual and attainment of the maturity of the race. The mature human being soon begins to look upon all other mortals with feelings of tenderness and with emotions of tolerance. Mature men view immature folks with the love and consideration that parents bear their children.

160:1.7 (1773.4) Successful living is nothing more or less than the art of the mastery of dependable techniques for solving common problems. The first step in the solution of any problem is to locate the difficulty, to isolate the problem, and frankly to recognize its nature and gravity. The great mistake is that, when life problems excite our profound fears, we refuse to recognize them. Likewise, when the acknowledgment of our difficulties entails the reduction of our long- cherished conceit, the admission of envy, or the abandonment of deep-seated prejudices, the average person prefers to cling to the old illusions of safety and to the long-cherished false feelings of security. Only a brave person is willing honestly to admit, and fearlessly to face, what a sincere and logical mind discovers.

160:1.8 (1773.5) The wise and effective solution of any problem demands that the mind shall be free from bias, passion, and all other purely personal prejudices which might interfere with the disinterested survey of the actual factors that go to make up the problem presenting itself for solution. The solution of life problems requires courage and sincerity. Only honest and brave individuals are able to follow valiantly through the perplexing and confusing maze of living to where the logic of a fearless mind may lead. And this emancipation of the mind and soul can never be effected without the driving power of an intelligent enthusiasm which borders on religious zeal. It requires the lure of a great ideal to drive man on in the pursuit of a goal which is beset with difficult material problems and manifold intellectual hazards.

160:1.9 (1774.1) Even though you are effectively armed to meet the difficult situations of life, you can hardly expect success unless you are equipped with that wisdom of mind and charm of personality which enable you to win the hearty support and co-operation of your fellows. You cannot hope for a large measure of success in either secular or religious work unless you can learn how to persuade your fellows, to prevail with men. You simply must have tact and tolerance.

160:1.10 (1774.2) But the greatest of all methods of problem solving I have learned from Jesus, your Master. I refer to that which he so consistently practices, and which he has so faithfully taught you, the isolation of worshipful meditation. In this habit of Jesus' going off so frequently by himself to commune with the Father in heaven is to be found the technique, not only of gathering strength and wisdom for the ordinary conflicts of living, but also of appropriating the energy for the solution of the higher problems of a moral and spiritual nature. But even correct methods of solving problems will not compensate for inherent defects of personality or atone for the absence of the hunger and thirst for true righteousness.

160:1.11 (1774.3) I am deeply impressed with the custom of Jesus in going apart by himself to engage in these seasons of solitary survey of the problems of living; to seek for new stores of wisdom and energy for meeting the manifold demands of social service; to quicken and deepen the supreme purpose of living by actually subjecting the total personality to the consciousness of contacting with divinity; to grasp for possession of new and better methods of adjusting oneself to the ever-changing situations of living existence; to effect those vital reconstructions and readjustments of one's personal attitudes which are so essential to enhanced insight into everything worth while and real; and to do all of this with an eye single to the glory of God—to breathe in sincerity your Master's favorite prayer, "Not my will, but yours, be done."

160:1.12 (1774.4) This worshipful practice of your Master brings that relaxation which renews the mind; that illumination which inspires the soul; that courage which enables one bravely to face one's problems; that self-understanding which obliterates debilitating fear; and that consciousness of union with divinity which equips man with the assurance that enables him to dare to be Godlike. The relaxation of worship, or spiritual communion as practiced by the Master, relieves tension, removes conflicts, and mightily augments the total resources of the personality. And all this philosophy, plus the gospel of the kingdom, constitutes the new religion as I understand it.

160:1.13 (1774.5) Prejudice blinds the soul to the recognition of truth, and prejudice can be removed only by the sincere devotion of the soul to the adoration of a cause that is all-embracing and all-inclusive of one's fellow men. Prejudice is inseparably linked to selfishness. Prejudice can be eliminated only by the abandonment of self-seeking and by substituting therefor the quest of the satisfaction of the service of a cause that is not only greater than self, but one that is even greater than all humanity—the search for God, the attainment of divinity. The evidence of maturity of personality consists in the transformation of human desire so that it constantly seeks for the realization of those values which are highest and most divinely real.

160:1.14 (1774.6) In a continually changing world, in the midst of an evolving social order, it is impossible to maintain settled and established goals of destiny. Stability of personality can be experienced only by those who have discovered and embraced the living God as the eternal goal of infinite attainment. And thus to transfer one's goal from time to eternity, from earth to Paradise, from the human to the divine, requires that man shall become regenerated, converted, be born again; that he shall become the re-created child of the divine spirit; that he shall gain entrance into the brotherhood of the kingdom of heaven. All philosophies and religions which fall short of these ideals are immature. The philosophy which I teach, linked with the gospel which you preach, represents the new religion of maturity, the ideal of all future generations. And this is true because our ideal is final, infallible, eternal, universal, absolute, and infinite.

160:1.15 (1775.1) My philosophy gave me the urge to search for the realities of true attainment, the goal of maturity. But my urge was impotent; my search lacked driving power; my quest suffered from the absence of certainty of directionization. And these deficiencies have been abundantly supplied by this new gospel of Jesus, with its enhancement of insights, elevation of ideals, and settledness of goals. Without doubts and misgivings I can now wholeheartedly enter upon the eternal venture.

## 2. The Art of Living

160:2.1 (1775.2) There are just two ways in which mortals may live together: the material or animal way and the spiritual or human way. By the use of signals and sounds animals are able to communicate with each other in a limited way. But such forms of communication do not convey meanings, values, or ideas. The one distinction between man and the animal is that man can communicate with his fellows by means of symbols which most certainly designate and identify meanings, values, ideas, and even ideals.

160:2.2 (1775.3) Since animals cannot communicate ideas to each other, they cannot develop personality. Man develops personality because he can thus communicate with his fellows concerning both ideas and ideals.

160:2.3 (1775.4) It is this ability to communicate and share meanings that constitutes human culture and enables man, through social associations, to build civilizations. Knowledge and wisdom become cumulative because of man's ability to communicate these possessions to succeeding generations. And thereby arise the cultural activities of the race: art, science, religion, and philosophy.

160:2.4 (1775.5) Symbolic communication between human beings predetermines the bringing into existence of social groups. The most effective of all social groups is the family, more particularly the two parents. Personal affection is the spiritual bond which holds together these material associations. Such an effective relationship is also possible between two persons of the same sex, as is so abundantly illustrated in the devotions of genuine friendships.

160:2.5 (1775.6) These associations of friendship and mutual affection are socializing and ennobling because they encourage and facilitate the following essential factors of the higher levels of the art of living:

160:2.6 (1775.7) 1. Mutual self-expression and self-understanding. Many noble human impulses die because there is no one to hear their expression. Truly, it is not good for man to be alone. Some degree of recognition and a certain amount of appreciation are essential to the development of human character. Without the genuine love of a home, no child can achieve the full development of normal character. Character is something more than mere mind and morals. Of all social relations calculated to develop character, the most effective and ideal is the affectionate and understanding friendship of man and woman in the mutual embrace of intelligent wedlock. Marriage, with its manifold relations, is best designed to draw forth those precious impulses and those higher motives which are indispensable to the development of a strong character. I do not hesitate thus to glorify family life, for your Master has wisely chosen the father-child relationship as the very cornerstone of this new gospel of the kingdom. And such a matchless community of relationship, man and woman in the fond embrace of the highest ideals of time, is so valuable and satisfying an experience that it is worth any price, any sacrifice, requisite for its possession.

160:2.7 (1776.1) 2. Union of souls—the mobilization of wisdom. Every human being sooner or later acquires a certain concept of this world and a certain vision of the next. Now it is possible, through personality association, to unite these views of temporal existence and eternal prospects. Thus does the mind of one augment its spiritual values by gaining much of the insight of the other. In this way men enrich the soul by pooling their respective spiritual possessions. Likewise, in this same way, man is enabled to avoid that ever- present tendency to fall victim to distortion of vision, prejudice of viewpoint, and narrowness of judgment. Fear, envy, and conceit can be prevented only by intimate contact with other minds. I call your attention to the fact that the Master never sends you out alone to labor for the extension of the kingdom; he always sends you out two and two. And since wisdom is superknowledge, it follows that, in the union of wisdom, the social group, small or large, mutually shares all knowledge.

160:2.8 (1776.2) 3. The enthusiasm for living. Isolation tends to exhaust the energy charge of the soul. Association with one's fellows is essential to the renewal of the zest for life and is indispensable to the maintenance of the courage to fight those battles consequent upon the ascent to the higher levels of human living.

Friendship enhances the joys and glorifies the triumphs of life. Loving and intimate human associations tend to rob suffering of its sorrow and hardship of much of its bitterness. The presence of a friend enhances all beauty and exalts every goodness. By intelligent symbols man is able to quicken and enlarge the appreciative capacities of his friends. One of the crowning glories of human friendship is this power and possibility of the mutual stimulation of the imagination. Great spiritual power is inherent in the consciousness of wholehearted devotion to a common cause, mutual loyalty to a cosmic Deity.

160:2.9 (1776.3) 4. The enhanced defense against all evil. Personality association and mutual affection is an efficient insurance against evil. Difficulties, sorrow, disappointment, and defeat are more painful and disheartening when borne alone. Association does not transmute evil into righteousness, but it does aid in greatly lessening the sting. Said your Master, "Happy are they who mourn"—if a friend is at hand to comfort. There is positive strength in the knowledge that you live for the welfare of others, and that these others likewise live for your welfare and advancement. Man languishes in isolation. Human beings unfailingly become discouraged when they view only the transitory transactions of time. The present, when divorced from the past and the future, becomes exasperatingly trivial. Only a glimpse of the circle of eternity can inspire man to do his best and can challenge the best in him to do its utmost. And when man is thus at his best, he lives most unselfishly for the good of others, his fellow sojourners in time and eternity.

160:2.10 (1777.1) I repeat, such inspiring and ennobling association finds its ideal possibilities in the human marriage relation. True, much is attained out of marriage, and many, many marriages utterly fail to produce these moral and spiritual fruits. Too many times marriage is entered by those who seek other values which are lower than these superior accompaniments of human maturity. Ideal marriage must be founded on something more stable than the fluctuations of sentiment and the fickleness of mere sex attraction; it must be based on genuine and mutual personal devotion. And thus, if you can build up such trustworthy and effective small units of human association, when these are assembled in the aggregate, the world will behold a great and glorified social structure, the civilization of mortal maturity. Such a race might begin to realize something of your Master's ideal of "peace on earth and good will among men." While such a society would not be perfect or entirely free from evil, it would at least approach the stabilization of maturity.

3. The Lures of Maturity

160:3.1 (1777.2) The effort toward maturity necessitates work, and work requires energy. Whence the power to accomplish all this? The physical things can be taken for granted, but the Master has well said, "Man cannot live by bread alone." Granted the possession of a normal body and reasonably good health, we must next look for those lures which will act as a stimulus to call forth man's slumbering spiritual forces. Jesus has taught us that God lives in man; then how can we induce man to release these soul-bound powers of divinity and infinity? How shall we induce men to let go of God that he may spring forth to the refreshment of our own souls while in transit outward and then to serve the purpose of enlightening, uplifting, and blessing countless other souls? How best can I awaken these latent powers for good which lie dormant in your souls? One thing I am sure of: Emotional excitement is not the ideal spiritual stimulus. Excitement does not augment energy; it rather exhausts the powers of both mind and body. Whence then comes the energy to do these great things? Look to your Master. Even now he is out in the hills taking in power while we are here giving out energy. The secret of all this problem is wrapped up in spiritual communion, in worship. From the human standpoint it is a question of combined meditation and relaxation. Meditation makes the contact of mind with spirit; relaxation determines the capacity for spiritual receptivity. And this interchange of strength for weakness, courage for fear, the will of God for the mind of self, constitutes worship. At least, that is the way the philosopher views it.

160:3.2 (1777.3) When these experiences are frequently repeated, they crystallize into habits, strength-giving and worshipful habits, and such habits eventually formulate themselves into a spiritual character, and such a character is finally recognized by one's fellows as a mature personality. These practices are difficult and time-consuming at first, but when they become habitual, they are at once restful and timesaving. The more complex society becomes, and the more the lures of civilization multiply, the more urgent will become the necessity for God-knowing individuals to form such protective habitual practices designed to conserve and augment their spiritual energies. *

160:3.3 (1778.1) Another requirement for the attainment of maturity is the co-operative adjustment of social groups to an ever-changing environment. The immature individual arouses the antagonisms of his fellows; the mature man wins the hearty co-operation of his associates, thereby many times multiplying the fruits of his life efforts.

160:3.4 (1778.2) My philosophy tells me that there are times when I must fight, if need be, for the defense of my concept of righteousness, but I doubt not that the Master, with a more mature type of personality, would easily and gracefully gain an equal victory by his superior and winsome technique of tact and tolerance. All too often, when we battle for the right, it turns out that both the victor and the vanquished have sustained defeat. I heard the Master say only yesterday that the "wise man, when seeking entrance through the locked door, would not destroy the door but rather would seek for the key wherewith to unlock it." Too often we engage in a fight merely to convince ourselves that we are not afraid.

160:3.5 (1778.3) This new gospel of the kingdom renders a great service to the art of living in that it supplies a new and richer incentive for higher living. It presents a new and exalted goal of destiny, a supreme life purpose. And these new concepts of the eternal and divine goal of existence are in themselves transcendent stimuli, calling forth the reaction of the very best that is resident in man's higher nature. On every mountaintop of intellectual thought are to be found relaxation for the mind, strength for the soul, and communion for the spirit. From such vantage points of high living, man is able to transcend the material irritations of the lower levels of thinking—worry, jealousy, envy, revenge, and the pride of immature personality. These high-climbing souls deliver themselves from a multitude of the crosscurrent conflicts of the trifles of living, thus becoming free to attain consciousness of the higher currents of spirit concept and celestial communication. But the life purpose must be jealously guarded from the temptation to seek for easy and transient attainment; likewise must it be so fostered as to become immune to the disastrous threats of fanaticism.

### 4. The Balance of Maturity

160:4.1 (1778.4) While you have an eye single to the attainment of eternal realities, you must also make provision for the necessities of temporal living. While the spirit is our goal, the flesh is a fact. Occasionally the necessities of living may fall into our hands by accident, but in general, we must intelligently work for them. The two major problems of life are: making a temporal living and the achievement of eternal survival. And even the problem of making a living requires religion for its ideal solution. These are both highly personal problems. True religion, in fact, does not function apart from the individual.

160:4.2 (1778.5) The essentials of the temporal life, as I see them, are:
160:4.3 (1778.6) 1. Good physical health.
160:4.4 (1778.7) 2. Clear and clean thinking.
160:4.5 (1778.8) 3. Ability and skill.

160:4.6 (1778.9) 4. Wealth—the goods of life.

160:4.7 (1778.10) 5. Ability to withstand defeat.

160:4.8 (1778.11) 6. Culture—education and wisdom.

160:4.9 (1779.1) Even the physical problems of bodily health and efficiency are best solved when they are viewed from the religious standpoint of our Master's teaching: That the body and mind of man are the dwelling place of the gift of the Gods, the spirit of God becoming the spirit of man. The mind of man thus becomes the mediator between material things and spiritual realities.

160:4.10 (1779.2) It requires intelligence to secure one's share of the desirable things of life. It is wholly erroneous to suppose that faithfulness in doing one's daily work will insure the rewards of wealth. Barring the occasional and accidental acquirement of wealth, the material rewards of the temporal life are found to flow in certain well-organized channels, and only those who have access to these channels may expect to be well rewarded for their temporal efforts. Poverty must ever be the lot of all men who seek for wealth in isolated and individual channels. Wise planning, therefore, becomes the one thing essential to worldly prosperity. Success requires not only devotion to one's work but also that one should function as a part of some one of the channels of material wealth. If you are unwise, you can bestow a devoted life upon your generation without material reward; if you are an accidental beneficiary of the flow of wealth, you may roll in luxury even though you have done nothing worth while for your fellow men.

160:4.11 (1779.3) Ability is that which you inherit, while skill is what you acquire. Life is not real to one who cannot do some one thing well, expertly. Skill is one of the real sources of the satisfaction of living. Ability implies the gift of foresight, farseeing vision. Be not deceived by the tempting rewards of dishonest achievement; be willing to toil for the later returns inherent in honest endeavor. The wise man is able to distinguish between means and ends; otherwise, sometimes overplanning for the future defeats its own high purpose. As a pleasure seeker you should aim always to be a producer as well as a consumer.

160:4.12 (1779.4) Train your memory to hold in sacred trust the strength-giving and worth-while episodes of life, which you can recall at will for your pleasure and edification. Thus build up for yourself and in yourself reserve galleries of beauty, goodness, and artistic grandeur. But the noblest of all memories are the treasured recollections of the great moments of a superb friendship. And all of these memory treasures radiate their most precious and exalting influences under the releasing touch of spiritual worship.

160:4.13 (1779.5) But life will become a burden of existence unless you learn how to fail gracefully. There is an art in defeat which noble souls always acquire; you must know how to lose cheerfully; you must be fearless of disappointment. Never hesitate to admit failure. Make no attempt to hide failure under deceptive smiles and beaming optimism. It sounds well always to claim success, but the end results are appalling. Such a technique leads directly to the creation of a world of unreality and to the inevitable crash of ultimate disillusionment.

160:4.14 (1779.6) Success may generate courage and promote confidence, but wisdom comes only from the experiences of adjustment to the results of one's failures. Men who prefer optimistic illusions to reality can never become wise. Only those who face facts and adjust them to ideals can achieve wisdom. Wisdom embraces both the fact and the ideal and therefore saves its devotees from both of those barren extremes of philosophy—the man whose idealism excludes facts and the materialist who is devoid of spiritual outlook. Those timid souls who can only keep up the struggle of life by the aid of continuous false illusions of success are doomed to suffer failure and experience defeat as they ultimately awaken from the dream world of their own imaginations.

160:4.15 (1780.1) And it is in this business of facing failure and adjusting to defeat that the far-reaching vision of religion exerts its supreme influence. Failure is simply an educational episode—a cultural experiment in the acquirement of wisdom—in the experience of the God-seeking man who has embarked on the eternal adventure of the exploration of a universe. To such men defeat is but a new tool for the achievement of higher levels of universe reality.

160:4.16 (1780.2) The career of a God-seeking man may prove to be a great success in the light of eternity, even though the whole temporal-life enterprise may appear as an overwhelming failure, provided each life failure yielded the culture of wisdom and spirit achievement. Do not make the mistake of confusing knowledge, culture, and wisdom. They are related in life, but they represent vastly differing spirit values; wisdom ever dominates knowledge and always glorifies culture.

5. The Religion of the Ideal

160:5.1 (1780.3) You have told me that your Master regards genuine human religion as the individual's experience with spiritual realities. I have regarded religion as man's experience of reacting to something which he regards as being worthy of the homage and devotion of all mankind. In this sense, religion symbolizes our supreme devotion to that which represents our highest concept of the ideals of reality and the farthest reach of our minds toward eternal possibilities of spiritual attainment.

160:5.2 (1780.4) When men react to religion in the tribal, national, or racial sense, it is because they look upon those without their group as not being truly human. We always look upon the object of our religious loyalty as being worthy of the reverence of all men. Religion can never be a matter of mere intellectual belief or philosophic reasoning; religion is always and forever a mode of reacting to the situations of life; it is a species of conduct. Religion embraces thinking, feeling, and acting reverently toward some reality which we deem worthy of universal adoration.

160:5.3 (1780.5) If something has become a religion in your experience, it is self-evident that you already have become an active evangel of that religion since you deem the supreme concept of your religion as being worthy of the worship of all mankind, all universe intelligences. If you are not a positive and missionary evangel of your religion, you are self- deceived in that what you call a religion is only a traditional belief or a mere system of intellectual philosophy. If your religion is a spiritual experience, your object of worship must be the universal spirit reality and ideal of all your spiritualized concepts. All religions based on fear, emotion, tradition, and philosophy I term the intellectual religions, while those based on true spirit experience I would term the true religions. The object of religious devotion may be material or spiritual, true or false, real or unreal, human or divine. Religions can therefore be either good or evil.

160:5.4 (1780.6) Morality and religion are not necessarily the same. A system of morals, by grasping an object of worship, may become a religion. A religion, by losing its universal appeal to loyalty and supreme devotion, may evolve into a system of philosophy or a code of morals. This thing, being, state, or order of existence, or possibility of attainment which constitutes the supreme ideal of religious loyalty, and which is the recipient of the religious devotion of those who worship, is God. Regardless of the name applied to this ideal of spirit reality, it is God.

160:5.5 (1781.1) The social characteristics of a true religion consist in the fact that it invariably seeks to convert the individual and to transform the world. Religion implies the existence of undiscovered ideals which far transcend the known standards of ethics and morality embodied in even the highest social usages of the most mature institutions of civilization. Religion reaches out for undiscovered ideals, unexplored realities, superhuman values, divine wisdom, and true spirit attainment. True religion does all of this; all other beliefs are not worthy of the name. You cannot have a genuine spiritual religion without the supreme and supernal ideal of an eternal God. A religion without this God is an invention of man, a human institution of lifeless intellectual beliefs and meaningless emotional ceremonies. A religion might claim as the object of its devotion a great ideal. But such ideals of unreality are not attainable; such a concept is illusionary. The only ideals susceptible of human attainment are the divine realities of the infinite values resident in the spiritual fact of the eternal God.

160:5.6 (1781.2) The word God, the idea of God as contrasted with the ideal of God, can become a part of any religion, no matter how puerile or false that religion may chance to be. And this idea of God can become anything which those who entertain it may choose to make it. The lower religions shape their ideas of God to meet the natural state of the human heart; the higher religions demand that the human heart shall be changed to meet the demands of the ideals of true religion.

160:5.7 (1781.3) The religion of Jesus transcends all our former concepts of the idea of worship in that he not only portrays his Father as the ideal of infinite reality but positively declares that this divine source of values and the eternal center of the universe is truly and personally attainable by every mortal creature who chooses to enter the kingdom of heaven on earth, thereby acknowledging the acceptance of sonship with God and brotherhood with man. That, I submit, is the highest concept of religion the world has ever known, and I pronounce that there can never be a higher since this gospel embraces the infinity of realities, the divinity of values, and the eternity of universal attainments. Such a concept constitutes the achievement of the experience of the idealism of the supreme and the ultimate.

160:5.8 (1781.4) I am not only intrigued by the consummate ideals of this religion of your Master, but I am mightily moved to profess my belief in his announcement that these ideals of spirit realities are attainable; that you and I can enter upon this long and eternal adventure with his assurance of the certainty of our ultimate arrival at the portals of Paradise. My brethren, I am a believer, I have embarked; I am on my way with you in this eternal venture. The Master says he came from the Father, and that he will show us the way. I am fully persuaded he speaks the truth. I am finally convinced that there are no attainable ideals of reality or values of perfection apart from the eternal and Universal Father.

160:5.9 (1781.5) I come, then, to worship, not merely the God of existences, but the God of the possibility of all future existences. Therefore must your devotion to a supreme ideal, if that ideal is real, be devotion to this God of past, present, and future universes of things and beings. And there is no other God, for there cannot possibly be any other God. All other gods are figments of the imagination, illusions of mortal mind, distortions of false logic, and the self- deceptive idols of those who create them. Yes, you can have a religion without this God, but it does not mean anything. And if you seek to substitute the word God for the reality of this ideal of the living God, you have only deluded yourself by putting an idea in the place of an ideal, a divine reality. Such beliefs are merely religions of wishful fancy.

160:5.10 (1782.1) I see in the teachings of Jesus, religion at its best. This gospel enables us to seek for the true God and to find him. But are we willing to pay the price of this entrance into the kingdom of heaven? Are we willing to be born again? to be remade? Are we willing to be subject to this terrible and testing process of self-destruction and soul reconstruction? Has not the Master said: "Whoso would save his life must lose it. Think not that I have come to bring peace but rather a soul struggle"? True, after we pay the price of dedication to the Father's will, we do experience great peace provided we continue to walk in these spiritual paths of consecrated living.

160:5.11 (1782.2) Now are we truly forsaking the lures of the known order of existence while we unreservedly dedicate our quest to the lures of the unknown and unexplored order of the existence of a future life of adventure in the spirit worlds of the higher idealism of divine reality. And we seek for those symbols of meaning wherewith to convey to our fellow men these concepts of the reality of the idealism of the religion of Jesus, and we will not cease to pray for that day when all mankind shall be thrilled by the communal vision of this supreme truth. Just now, our focalized concept of the Father, as held in our hearts, is that God is spirit; as conveyed to our fellows, that God is love.

160:5.12 (1782.3) The religion of Jesus demands living and spiritual experience. Other religions may consist in traditional beliefs, emotional feelings, philosophic consciousness, and all of that, but the teaching of the Master requires the attainment of actual levels of real spirit progression.

160:5.13 (1782.4) The consciousness of the impulse to be like God is not true religion. The feelings of the emotion to worship God are not true religion. The knowledge of the conviction to forsake self and serve God is not true religion. The wisdom of the reasoning that this religion is the best of all is not religion as a personal and spiritual experience. True religion has reference to destiny and reality of attainment as well as to the reality and idealism of that which is wholeheartedly faith-accepted. And all of this must be made personal to us by the revelation of the Spirit of Truth.

160:5.14 (1782.5) And thus ended the dissertations of the Greek philosopher, one of the greatest of his race, who had become a believer in the gospel of Jesus.

## Paper 161
## Further Discussions with Rodan

161:0.1 (1783.1) ON SUNDAY, September 25, A.D. 29, the apostles and the evangelists assembled at Magadan. After a long conference that evening with his associates, Jesus surprised all by announcing that early the next day he and the twelve apostles would start for Jerusalem to attend the feast of tabernacles. He directed that the evangelists visit the believers in Galilee, and that the women's corps return for a while to Bethsaida.

161:0.2 (1783.2) When the hour came to leave for Jerusalem, Nathaniel and Thomas were still in the midst of their discussions with Rodan of Alexandria, and they secured the Master's permission to remain at Magadan for a few days. And so, while Jesus and the ten were on their way to Jerusalem, Nathaniel and Thomas were engaged in earnest debate with Rodan. The week prior, in which Rodan had expounded his philosophy, Thomas and Nathaniel had alternated in presenting the gospel of the kingdom to the Greek philosopher. Rodan discovered that he had been well instructed in Jesus' teachings by one of the former apostles of John the Baptist who had been his teacher at Alexandria.

### 1. The Personality of God

161:1.1 (1783.3) There was one matter on which Rodan and the two apostles did not see alike, and that was the personality of God. Rodan readily accepted all that was presented to him regarding the attributes of God, but he contended that the Father in heaven is not, cannot be, a person as man conceives personality. While the apostles found themselves in difficulty trying to prove that God is a person, Rodan found it still more difficult to prove he is not a person.

161:1.2 (1783.4) Rodan contended that the fact of personality consists in the coexistent fact of full and mutual communication between beings of equality, beings who are capable of sympathetic understanding. Said Rodan: "In order to be a person, God must have symbols of spirit communication which would enable him to become fully understood by those who make contact with him. But since God is infinite and eternal, the Creator of all other beings, it follows that, as regards beings of equality, God is alone in the universe. There are none equal to him; there are none with whom he can communicate as an equal. God indeed may be the source of all personality, but as such he is transcendent to personality, even as the Creator is above and beyond the creature."

161:1.3 (1783.5) This contention greatly troubled Thomas and Nathaniel, and they had asked Jesus to come to their rescue, but the Master refused to enter into their discussions. He did say to Thomas: "It matters little what idea of the Father you may entertain as long as you are spiritually acquainted with the ideal of his infinite and eternal nature."

161:1.4 (1784.1) Thomas contended that God does communicate with man, and therefore that the Father is a person, even within the definition of Rodan. This the Greek rejected on the ground that God does not reveal himself personally; that he is still a mystery. Then Nathaniel appealed to his own personal experience with God, and that Rodan allowed, affirming that he had recently had similar experiences, but these experiences, he contended, proved only the reality of God, not his personality.

161:1.5 (1784.2) By Monday night Thomas gave up. But by Tuesday night Nathaniel had won Rodan to believe in the personality of the Father, and he effected this change in the Greek's views by the following steps of reasoning:

161:1.6 (1784.3) 1. The Father in Paradise does enjoy equality of communication with at least two other beings who are fully equal to himself and wholly like himself—the Eternal Son and the Infinite Spirit. In view of the doctrine of the Trinity, the Greek was compelled to concede the personality possibility of the Universal Father. (It was the later consideration of these discussions which led to the enlarged conception of the Trinity in the minds of the twelve apostles. Of course, it was the general belief that Jesus was the Eternal Son.)

161:1.7 (1784.4) 2. Since Jesus was equal with the Father, and since this Son had achieved the manifestation of personality to his earth children, such a phenomenon constituted proof of the fact, and demonstration of the possibility, of the possession of personality by all three of the Godheads and forever settled the question regarding the ability of God to communicate with man and the possibility of man's communicating with God.

161:1.8 (1784.5) 3. That Jesus was on terms of mutual association and perfect communication with man; that Jesus was the Son of God. That the relation of Son and Father presupposes equality of communication and mutuality of sympathetic understanding; that Jesus and the Father were one. That Jesus maintained at one and the same time understanding communication with both God and man, and that, since both God and man comprehended the meaning of the symbols of Jesus' communication, both God and man possessed the attributes of personality in so far as the requirements of the ability of intercommunication were concerned. That the personality of Jesus demonstrated the personality of God, while it proved conclusively the presence of God in man. That two things which are related to the same thing are related to each other.

161:1.9 (1784.6) 4. That personality represents man's highest concept of human reality and divine values; that God also represents man's highest concept of divine reality and infinite values; therefore, that God must be a divine and infinite personality, a personality in reality although infinitely and eternally transcending man's concept and definition of personality, but nevertheless always and universally a personality.

161:1.10 (1784.7) 5. That God must be a personality since he is the Creator of all personality and the destiny of all personality. Rodan had been tremendously influenced by the teaching of Jesus, "Be you therefore perfect, even as your Father in heaven is perfect."

161:1.11 (1784.8) When Rodan heard these arguments, he said: "I am convinced. I will confess God as a person if you will permit me to qualify my confession of such a belief by attaching to the meaning of personality a group of extended values, such as superhuman, transcendent, supreme, infinite, eternal, final, and universal. I am now convinced that, while God must be infinitely more than a personality, he cannot be anything less. I am satisfied to end the argument and to accept Jesus as the personal revelation of the Father and the satisfaction of all unsatisfied factors in logic, reason, and philosophy."

## 2. The Divine Nature of Jesus

161:2.1 (1785.1) Since Nathaniel and Thomas had so fully approved Rodan's views of the gospel of the kingdom, there remained only one more point to consider, the teaching dealing with the divine nature of Jesus, a doctrine only so recently publicly announced. Nathaniel and Thomas jointly presented their views of the divine nature of the Master, and the following narrative is a condensed, rearranged, and restated presentation of their teaching:

161:2.2 (1785.2) 1. Jesus has admitted his divinity, and we believe him. Many remarkable things have happened in connection with his ministry which we can understand only by believing that he is the Son of God as well as the Son of Man.

161:2.3 (1785.3) 2. His life association with us exemplifies the ideal of human friendship; only a divine being could possibly be such a human friend. He is the most truly unselfish person we have ever known. He is the friend even of sinners; he dares to love his enemies. He is very loyal to us. While he does not hesitate to reprove us, it is plain to all that he truly loves us. The better you know him, the more you will love him. You will be charmed by his unswerving devotion. Through all these years of our failure to comprehend his mission, he has been a faithful friend. While he makes no use of flattery, he does treat us all with equal kindness; he is invariably tender and compassionate. He has shared his life and everything else with us. We are a happy community; we share all things in common. We do not believe that a mere human could live such a blameless life under such trying circumstances.

161:2.4 (1785.4) 3. We think Jesus is divine because he never does wrong; he makes no mistakes. His wisdom is extraordinary; his piety superb. He lives day by day in perfect accord with the Father's will. He never repents of misdeeds because he transgresses none of the Father's laws. He prays for us and with us, but he never asks us to pray for him. We believe that he is consistently sinless. We do not think that one who is only human ever professed to live such a life. He claims to live a perfect life, and we acknowledge that he does. Our piety springs from repentance, but his piety springs from righteousness. He even professes to forgive sins and does heal diseases. No mere man would sanely profess to forgive sin; that is a divine prerogative. And he has seemed to be thus perfect in his righteousness from the times of our first contact with him. We grow in grace and in the knowledge of the truth, but our Master exhibits maturity of righteousness to start with. All men, good and evil, recognize these elements of goodness in Jesus. And yet never is his piety obtrusive or ostentatious. He is both meek and fearless. He seems to approve of our belief in his divinity. He is either what he professes to be, or else he is the greatest hypocrite and fraud the world has ever known. We are persuaded that he is just what he claims to be.

161:2.5 (1785.5) 4. The uniqueness of his character and the perfection of his emotional control convince us that he is a combination of humanity and divinity. He unfailingly responds to the spectacle of human need; suffering never fails to appeal to him. His compassion is moved alike by physical suffering, mental anguish, or spiritual sorrow. He is quick to recognize and generous to acknowledge the presence of faith or any other grace in his fellow men. He is so just and fair and at the same time so merciful and considerate. He grieves over the spiritual obstinacy of the people and rejoices when they consent to see the light of truth.

161:2.6 (1786.1) 5. He seems to know the thoughts of men's minds and to understand the longings of their hearts. And he is always sympathetic with our troubled spirits. He seems to possess all our human emotions, but they are magnificently glorified. He strongly loves goodness and equally hates sin. He possesses a superhuman consciousness of the presence of Deity. He prays like a man but performs like a God. He seems to foreknow things; he even now dares to speak about his death, some mystic reference to his future glorification. While he is kind, he is also brave and courageous. He never falters in doing his duty.

161:2.7 (1786.2) 6. We are constantly impressed by the phenomenon of his superhuman knowledge. Hardly does a day pass but something transpires to disclose that the Master knows what is going on away from his immediate presence. He also seems to know about the thoughts of his associates. He undoubtedly has communion with celestial personalities; he unquestionably lives on a spiritual plane far above the rest of us. Everything seems to be open to his unique understanding. He asks us questions to draw us out, not to gain information.

161:2.8 (1786.3) 7. Recently the Master does not hesitate to assert his superhumanity. From the day of our ordination as apostles right on down to recent times, he has never denied that he came from the Father above. He speaks with the authority of a divine teacher. The Master does not hesitate to refute the religious teachings of today and to declare the new gospel with positive authority. He is assertive, positive, and authoritative. Even John the Baptist, when he heard Jesus speak, declared that he was the Son of God. He seems to be so sufficient within himself. He craves not the support of the multitude; he is indifferent to the opinions of men. He is brave and yet so free from pride.

161:2.9 (1786.4) 8. He constantly talks about God as an ever-present associate in all that he does. He goes about doing good, for God seems to be in him. He makes the most astounding assertions about himself and his mission on earth, statements which would be absurd if he were not divine. He once declared, "Before Abraham was, I am." He has definitely claimed divinity; he professes to be in partnership with God. He well-nigh exhausts the possibilities of language in the reiteration of his claims of intimate association with the heavenly Father. He even dares to assert that he and the Father are one. He says that anyone who has seen him has seen the Father. And he says and does all these tremendous things with such childlike naturalness. He alludes to his association with the Father in the same manner that he refers to his association with us. He seems to be so sure about God and speaks of these relations in such a matter-of-fact way. *

161:2.10 (1786.5) 9. In his prayer life he appears to communicate directly with his Father. We have heard few of his prayers, but these few would indicate that he talks with God, as it were, face to face. He seems to know the future as well as the past. He simply could not be all of this and do all of these extraordinary things unless he were something more than human. We know he is human, we are sure of that, but we are almost equally sure that he is also divine. We believe that he is divine. We are convinced that he is the Son of Man and the Son of God.

161:2.11 (1787.1) When Nathaniel and Thomas had concluded their conferences with Rodan, they hurried on toward Jerusalem to join their fellow apostles, arriving on Friday of that week. This had been a great experience in the lives of all three of these believers, and the other apostles learned much from the recounting of these experiences by Nathaniel and Thomas.

161:2.12 (1787.2) Rodan made his way back to Alexandria, where he long taught his philosophy in the school of Meganta. He became a mighty man in the later affairs of the kingdom of heaven; he was a faithful believer to the end of his earth days, yielding up his life in Greece with others when the persecutions were at their height.

3. Jesus' Human and Divine Minds

161:3.1 (1787.3) Consciousness of divinity was a gradual growth in the mind of Jesus up to the occasion of his baptism. After he became fully self-conscious of his divine nature, prehuman existence, and universe prerogatives, he seems to have possessed the power of variously limiting his human consciousness of his divinity. It appears to us that from his baptism until the crucifixion it was entirely optional with Jesus whether to depend only on the human mind or to utilize the knowledge of both the human and the divine minds. At times he appeared to avail himself of only that information which was resident in the human intellect. On other occasions he appeared to act with such fullness of knowledge and wisdom as could be afforded only by the utilization of the superhuman content of his divine consciousness.

161:3.2 (1787.4) We can understand his unique performances only by accepting the theory that he could, at will, self-limit his divinity consciousness. We are fully cognizant that he frequently withheld from his associates his foreknowledge of events, and that he was aware of the nature of their thinking and planning. We understand that he did not wish his followers to know too fully that he was able to discern their thoughts and to penetrate their plans. He did not desire too far to transcend the concept of the human as it was held in the minds of his apostles and disciples.

161:3.3 (1787.5) We are utterly at a loss to differentiate between his practice of self-limiting his divine consciousness and his technique of concealing his preknowledge and thought discernment from his human associates. We are convinced that he used both of these techniques, but we are not always able, in a given instance, to specify which method he may have employed. We frequently observed him acting with only the human content of consciousness; then would we behold him in conference with the directors of the celestial hosts of the universe and discern the undoubted functioning of the divine mind. And then on almost numberless occasions did we witness the working of this combined personality of man and God as it was activated by the apparent perfect union of the human and the divine minds. This is the limit of our knowledge of such phenomena; we really do not actually know the full truth about this mystery.

Made in the USA
Middletown, DE
06 June 2024

55436744R00029